Summary of

Good Profit

by Charles G. Koch

Instaread

Please Note

This is a key takeaways and analysis.

Table of Contents

Overview

Good Profit: How Creating Value for Others Built One of the World's Most Successful Companies is a nonfiction book that outlines the management strategy of Charles G. Koch, the chief executive officer (CEO) of Koch Industries, Inc. It builds on his 2007 book, *The Science of Success: How Market-Based Management Built the World's Largest Private Company*, by including guidance on how to apply his management strategies, and answers questions about Koch Industries's success and failures.

Good profit occurs when a company generates value for customers by offering the best goods or services at the best price using the smallest amount of resources and helps people improve their lives. Good profit comes from products that are innovative, that come from creative destruction, and are sometimes products the customers did not know they needed. These products create good profit because customers vote with their dollars. Good profit also results from business choices that are good in the long term for the business, as well as the customer and society as a whole.

In order to create good profit, Koch has used and honed, since the mid-1960s, a management framework called Market-Based Management (MBM). MBM helps a business know what it should do to create the most value in a society and, therefore, generate good profit for the business. MBM works on five dimensions: vision, virtue and talent, knowledge processes, decision rights, and incentives.

Important People

Charles G. Koch: Charles G. Koch is co-owner, chairman, and CEO of Koch Industries, Inc, and the author of *The Science of Success*, a book that is also about MBM. He was ranked the ninth richest person in the world in 2014, and is also a prominent philanthropist and Libertarian.

David H. Koch: David H. Koch is Charles's younger brother and executive vice president of Koch Industries. He is a prolific philanthropist, has given to Memorial Sloan Kettering and Lincoln Center, and is a Libertarian and former Libertarian vice presidential candidate.

Fred C. Koch: Fred C. Koch, the son of a Dutch immigrant, was an engineer and entrepreneur. He started the oil refinery company, Rock Island Oil and Refining, that became Koch Industries.

Joseph Schumpeter: Joseph Schumpeter was an Austrian-American economist. He popularized the idea of creative destruction, which is an instrumental concept in the MBM philosophy.

Adam Smith: Adam Smith was an eighteenth century philosopher who created modern economic theory. He introduced the concept of the invisible hand, where people's self-interest creates a successful and prosperous economy in a free market system.

W. Edwards Deming: W. Edwards Deming was an American management consultant. He introduced a theory of management that relies on constant improvement and innovation that Koch used as part of the basis for MBM.

Sterling Varner: Sterling Varner served as Koch Industries vice chairman and president. He was born in a tent in Texas, and rose to become a successful businessman and good friend of Charles Koch.

Key Takeaways

1. Adversity is the key to success.

2. Corporate welfare in the form of handouts and tax subsidies obscures the free market and is negative for the economy.

3. The customer, and society in general, are not groups that should be cheated for a profit. Instead, good profit arises from a win-win situation where the customer benefits as well.

4. A company's vision and mission statement is the cornerstone of good management.

5. Companies must hire by looking first for virtues that align with a company. Talent has less to do with a specific job title and more with what competitive advantages and strengths potential employees offer.

6. Strong communication is essential for success. Companies must foster an environment where subordinates can communicate openly with their managers.

7. In order for a company to succeed, employees must feel as though they are responsible for their work and have agency. This improves accountability and results.

8. Creating thoughtful incentives both in the long and short term as well as financial and non-financial ways, where each employee has unlimited potential to earn, motivates employees.

9. In order to work, the Market-Based Management (MBM) system needs to be adopted wholesale.

Thank you for purchasing this Instaread book

**Download the Instaread mobile app to get
unlimited text & audio summaries
of bestselling books.**

Visit Instaread.co
to learn more.

Analysis

Key Takeaway 1

Adversity is the key to success.

Analysis

Fred Koch taught Charles Koch that adversity is actually a blessing and failure builds character. Charles took this to heart, especially when he did not succeed in school or professionally. When a Koch Industries pipeline burst in Texas in 1996, killing two teenagers, Koch applied the lessons of the horrible tragedy to the way Koch Industries dealt with government regulation and pipeline maintenance.

Especially in a business climate where nine out of ten startups fail, the idea of learning from failure in business has never been more important. In the 2014 book, *The Upside of Down: Why Failing Well Is the Key to Success,* popular business blogger Megan McArdle argues that people will fail, but to succeed they need to learn to harness the power of their failure and identify the failure early to turn it into success. Through her research in science, psychology, business, and economics, as well as interviews with emergency room doctors and venture capitalists, she came to the conclusion that failure is how people learn. McArdle also argues that this ability is a distinctly US phenomenon. In the United States, failure and reinvention are especially tolerated [1].

Koch's point of view echoes McArdle's in a few respects. First of all, he believes that, although failure is important, the risks need to be recognized so the failure is on the correct scale. He also believes that it is important to business and personal growth, and it does not penalize employees for taking risks.

Key Takeaway 2

Corporate welfare in the forms of handouts and tax subsidies obscures the free market and is negative for the economy.

Analysis

For companies to make good profit, the incentives for customers cannot be obscured by government intervention, such as bailouts and tax subsidies. This prevents the win-win situation and relationship that allows the best companies to connect with customers and better the world.

A recent example of government intervention is the solar panel manufacturer Solyndra. In 2011, Solyndra defaulted on a $535 million loan provided by the Department of Energy for green energy projects. Even though green initiatives seem good in theory, there is evidence that Solyndra did not deserve the government's money. According to an energy department report, Solyndra misled the government about the value of the commitments it had as well as knowingly overestimating the premium it could charge for its panels [2]. Solyndra would not have been a successful company in the free market and the effect of the loan default was a loss of US taxpayer money as well as a lack of trust in further green power initiatives. This type of propping up destroys the free market and changes the relationship with customers a company has. A better way to create cleaner power is to allow the market to push companies to innovate new solutions that satisfy customers as well as become better with resources in order to create good profit.

Key Takeaway 3

The customer, and society in general, are not groups that should be cheated for a profit. Instead, good profit arises from a win-win situation where the customer benefits as well.

Analysis

At a Koch Industries meeting in the 1970s, some employees were laughing about how they had outsmarted a customer because the deal was so favorable for Koch Industries. Sterling Varner yelled at the employees, telling them that they were out of line, because the customers are the ones who keep them in business and are to be considered friends.

Nancy Michaels, a business coach and consultant, points out that life is relationship based, so business should be as well. People put a high value on the people they are close to and their relationships with them. In business, if people focus on the clients and customers this way, they will have a greater impact. "I'm a firm believer in creating win-win-win scenarios for the people I serve," Michaels told the *Huffington Post*. "I want to offer a quality service at a fair price that will have five times the value to my clients as what I'm charging. If they're happy, I'm happy." Michaels advises her clients to show an interest greater than the money they are exchanging for the good or service to the customer. It is more than about money. It is about how one can positively impact their lives [3]. This is win-win.

It is important to note that many people conceive of the idea of profit as bad. If they are making a profit, they are swindling the consumer. This is not always true.

Key Takeaway 4

A company's vision and mission statement is the cornerstone of good management.

Analysis

The Market-Based Management (MBM) strategy begins with a vision for the company. For Koch, this vision is providing competitive products and services that are better than the alternative and efficiently use resources. They strive to profit from benefiting their customers and society as a whole. Every company will have a slightly different vision.

Vision is extremely important because it allows a company to be successful. Companies that are successful maintain a core purpose and values while adapting their strategies to an ever changing world. Vision ties these two things together and helps companies know what to maintain, what to change, and how to go about the changes. A good framework for a company's vision gets at both the ideology and envisioned future of a company [4]. In the case of Koch Industries, the ideology of benefiting society informs the envisioned future, which is to constantly innovate and creatively destruct, in order to anticipate how to be the best in a changing world and improve the lives of their customers. The vision statement is a bedrock in a business such as Koch Industries that is constantly in flux as it acquires new companies with different existing management systems. If the company is a bricklayer, the vision tells the company which brick to lay next.

Key Takeaway 5

Companies must hire by looking first for virtues that align with the company's vision. Talent has less to do with a specific job title and more with what competitive advantages and strengths potential employees offer.

Analysis

It is much harder to teach values than skills. And a skilled employee with poor values that differ from those of the company the person works for is dangerous. So, when Koch Industries hire new employees, they hire for values first. Talent is important, but it it is not measured prescriptively by job title, but more by recognizing an individual's intelligence and aptitudes.

Koch Industries's complicated and thoughtful hiring process is extremely important to the company's growth. Businesses and their bottom lines are about people. A 2012 poll conducted by CareerBuilder found that 41 percent of participating companies experienced a $25,000 loss per single bad hire. Twenty-four percent experienced a $50,000 loss for a single bad hire. These negative hires add up. The reasons these hires did not work out seem to indicate that hiring is an important mix of values and talent. According to the same poll, 67 percent of the bad hires were bad because of their skills, and 60 percent were bad because of their inability to fit in with the company's culture. Hiring for core values is especially important with employees today because many want to feel as though their work is aligned with their own values. It is also important now because many startups do not have the brand-name recognition older companies do, so it is important to establish agreement around values. Hiring for values can be difficult, though, because many companies do not know the steps to take to do this and do not want to discriminate against potential hires [5]. But hiring for values has never been more important, especially when large technology companies with a widely known and understood culture are competitive in the hiring marketplace [6].

Koch Industries performs careful hiring with a highly selective multi-interview hiring process, and one that does not value big-city educations or long resumes over the right value system.

Key Takeaway 6

Strong communication is essential for success. Companies must foster an environment where subordinates can communicate openly with their managers.

Analysis

Companies and societies do best when knowledge is plentiful, accessible, and everyone has access to freedom of speech. In a non-business example, David Koch, Charles's brother, founded a cancer institute at the Massachusetts Institute of Technology (MIT) that thrives because the interdisciplinary researchers share advances in real time. Good knowledge processes include a myriad of communications that include communicating with outside analysts and consultants, communication within a company, utilizing the role of an IT department in fostering communication, and communication with the customer.

An especially important knowledge process is a culture where subordinate employees, especially those with specific real-time knowledge because they are on the ground, can share information with managers. Joseph Grenny, founder of a corporate training company, in an article in the Harvard Business Review, said, "You can approximate the effectiveness of the team — or even an entire organization — by measuring the average lag time between when problems are identified and when problems are brought out in the open." The article acknowledges that it is difficult to get people to speak up because people have an ingrained deference to authority and do not want to rock the boat. But encouraging this open communication can pay dividends. The people at the bottom have the best access to knowledge about what is happening on a day-to-day basis. An important way to encourage this behavior is to model it [7]. At Koch Industries, one way that communication is modeled is that employees have the opportunity to give Charles Koch feedback the way any employee would get it. He takes this feedback very seriously.

Key Takeaway 7

One way to improve accountability and results is to make employees feel as though they are responsible for their work and have agency.

Analysis

One way to get employees to actually communicate with each other and with their managers is to have them truly invested in the company. If they feel ownership and as though they can make a change, they will be more likely to speak up and take action, as opposed to acting like a cog in a wheel in a system they cannot change [8].

A feeling of ownership is extremely important to success. One historical example is the "tragedy of the commons." The term, and its related story, were first published in an 1833 essay written by the English economist William Forster Lloyd, and made popular in 1968 by economist Garrett Hardin. Everyone put their animals out to graze in a common pasture and the pasture was quickly run down. It happened because people had no incentive to control their animals. If they did not let their animals trample the field and eat all the grass, someone else would, so everyone did it. They had no investment in it. Compare this to a private pasture. The owner of the pasture had a vested interest in keeping the pasture maintained year after year, so that is what he did [9]. The same goes for an employee. If each employee has autonomy, room to grow, and basically is allowed to act as an entrepreneur in the their own part of the company, the employee will have a vested interest in the success of Koch Industries. People also want to feel as though their work is meaningful and lasting. Providing ownership helps with this [10].

Key Takeaway 8

Creating thoughtful incentives both in the long and short term as well as financial and nonfinancial ways, where each employee has unlimited potential to earn, motivates employees.

Analysis

Many existing corporate pay structures do not motivate employees in the long run or provide them with the ownership of their jobs that is necessary for them to do good work. For example, assigning base pay through hierarchy and awarding bonuses by group do little to motivate employees, especially in the long run. Base pay at Koch is considered an advance on what the employee will earn for the company.

Many companies pay out bonuses to employees who are not performing well. According to research by Towers Watson, a professional services company, 24 percent of companies in North America make annual incentive payouts to employees with low performance. Eighteen percent of companies do not base payouts on employee performance at all. Add in the practice of paying groups of employees all the same bonus and not paying attention to individual performance, and the pay system is not creating incentives for better performance and better performance over time. The money would be better off elsewhere in another part of the company [11]. However, in businesses, such as Koch Industries, employees with

proper incentives and carefully calculated pay are moti-
vated to do better work for a longer period of time. Also,
incentives are not just financial. Employees who see the
results of their work and who are praised for their abilities
will give more to their jobs [12].

Key Takeaway 9

In order to work, the Market-Based Management (MBM) system needs to be adopted wholesale.

Analysis

It is not easy to adhere to a successful management system. It has taken Koch Industries many years to hone theirs, with many setbacks and changes. Businesses need to be especially careful that the system permeates every part of the business and is put in action, instead of employees just paying lip service to the concepts or doing an analysis to please the CEO instead of seeing and understanding how that analysis contributes to the system.

Whether they use MBM or not, one thing most successful companies have in common is that they practice what they preach. Their ethos is not just symbolic, but is put into practice in every part of the business. The business might change but the ethos keeps it together. For example, Nike is synonymous with their slogan "Just Do It," and it is the identity they have honed over the years [13]. Sometimes a company missteps and does something that interferes with their core ethos. This can be so dramatic as to cause a change in the company's identity. For example, when Google transitioned into Alphabet, they dropped the motto "Don't Be Evil" from their basic code of conduct because some thought that the slogan was hypocritical and scared off advertisers. This shift signals a major change for the company [14].

Management systems only work if they are actually adopted on the ground. And they only work through trial and error. But the experience at Koch indicates the success of the MBM system. Although it is a lot of work for companies, it can create a successful business that grows and innovates every year.

Author's Style

Good Profit: How Creating Value for Others Built One of the World's Most Successful Companies by Charles Koch wears many hats in terms of style. There is a discourse on the advantages of a free market economy and the pitfalls of communism, and a refresher on economic theory. There are biographies of Fred, Charles, and David Koch, and the company as well, from its beginnings to its current multinational state. It also outlines the five principles of MBM in detail, relying on anecdotes from acquired companies and more general examples of economic theory. It then ends with case studies where the five principles are applied with success.

The book aims to show people of all kinds, including Koch Industries employees, business school students, small business owners, and stockholders how to implement MBM management. There were words and phrases that needed to be looked up for someone not fluent in business jargon or the oil refining business, but for someone with a familiarity with these it should be an easy read. Other sections, especially where material is summarized in bullet points, were easy-to-read takeaways, and could be applied in a business context easily. The case studies were very clear and compelling.

Building on his first book, *The Science of Success*, Koch promises to answer questions about Koch Industries, which comes under frequent fire from the media, and discuss his and his company's successes and shortcomings, warts and all. Although he speaks candidly about his desire to improve the world, and there are some poignant examples, such as an employee who named his son after Charles Koch because he was so inspired by the way the company was run, the book fails in this regard. He does not quite articulate how some of his routes to good profit actually improve society, beyond making Koch Industries a good company to work with or be a customer of. And, although he acknowledges them, the human and environmental pains of doing business, such as jobs lost through innovation, nitrogen pollution, a handful of accidents, and legal issues, get a quick gloss rather than a thoughtfully considered treatment.

Author's Perspective

Charles Koch is CEO, co-owner, and chairman of the board of Koch Industries. He lives in Wichita, Kansas, in the house he built many years ago when he returned to work for his father. In February 2014, he was ranked the ninth richest person in the world, at a net worth of $36 billion. Koch Industries is the second-largest privately held company in the United States. It is valued at over $100 billion and has over 100,000 employees all over the world. It has also won more than a thousand awards for safety, innovation, environmental stewardship, and other positive accomplishments since 2009. Koch is the author of *The Science of Success*, which is also about Market-Based Management [15].

Koch is a philanthropist. He gives to individuals and organizations that promote a free-market economy and he contributes to Republican and Libertarian groups and candidates. He co-founded the Cato Institute, a think tank dedicated to individual liberty. He also supports many nonprofits through the Charles Koch Foundation and the Charles Koch Institute. Through his wife, Elizabeth, he has also donated to the arts. [16] Koch sees himself as an honest midwesterner who betters his business and society as a whole through good management practices. In this book, he aims to share what has made Koch Industries so successful.

~~~~ END OF INSTAREAD ~~~~

Thank you for purchasing this Instaread book

**Download the Instaread mobile app to get
unlimited text & audio summaries
of bestselling books.**

Visit Instaread.co
to learn more.

References

1. McArdle, Megan. "The Upside of Down: Why Failing Well Is the Key to Success." *Amazon.com*, accessed November 11, 2015. http://www.amazon.com/The-Up-Side-Down-Failing-ebook/dp/B00DMCV4GM/ref=dp_kinw_strp_1

2. Howell, Kellan and Stephen Dinan. "Solyndra misled government to get $535M solar project loan: report." *Washington Times*, accessed November 11, 2015. www.washingtontimes.com/news/2015/aug/26/solyndra-misled-government-get-535-million-solar-p/

3. Michaels, Nancy. "Reinventing Win-Win-Win Business Relationships." *Huffington Post*, accessed November 11, 2015. http://www.huffingtonpost.com/nancy-michaels/reinventing-winwin-win-bus_b_6291030.html

4. Collins, Jim and Porras, Jerry I. "Building Your Company's Vision." *Harvard Business Review*, accessed November 11, 2015. https://hbr.org/1996/09/building-your-companys-vision

5. Wendy. "Hiring for Cultural Fit: Why it's Important and How to Go About It." *7Geese*, accessed November 11, 2015. http://7geese.com/hiring-for-cultural-fit-why-its-important-and-how-to-go-about-it/

6. Bersin, Josh. "Culture: Why It's The Hottest Topic In Business Today." *Forbes*, accessed November 11, 2015. http://www.forbes.com/sites/joshbersin/2015/03/13/culture-why-its-the-hottest-topic-in-business-today/

7. Knight, Rebecca. "How to Get Your Employees to Speak Up." *Harvard Business Review*, accessed November 11, 2015. https://hbr.org/2014/10/how-to-get-your-employees-to-speak-up/

8. Ibid.

9. "Tragedy of the commons." *Wikipedia.org*, accessed November 11, 2015. https://en.wikipedia.org/wiki/Tragedy_of_the_commons

10. Gross, Jessica. "What Motivates Us At Work? More Than Money." *Ideas.Ted.Com*, accessed November 11, 2015. http://ideas.ted.com/what-motivates-us-at-work-7-fascinating-studies-that-give-insights/

11. Sammer, Joanne. "Not an Entitlement: Keep Bonuses Performance-Based." *Society for Human Resource Management*, accessed November 11, 2015. http://www.shrm.org/hrdisciplines/compensation/articles/pages/performance-based-bonuses.aspx

12. Gross, Jessica. "What Motivates Us At Work? More Than Money." *Ideas.Ted.Com*, accessed

November 11, 2015. http://ideas.ted.com/what-motivates-us-at-work-7-fascinating-studies-that-give-insights/

13. Llopis, Glenn. "The Most Successful Companies Embrace the Promise of Their Culture." *Forbes*, accessed November 11, 2015. http://www.forbes.com/sites/glennllopis/2011/09/12/the-most-successful-companies-embrace-the-promise-of-their-culture/

14. Basu, Tanya. "New Google Parent Company Drops 'Don't Be Evil' Motto." *Time*, accessed November 11, 2015. http://time.com/4060575/alphabet-google-dont-be-evil/

15. "The Science of Success: How Market-Based Management Built the World's Largest Private Company." *Amazon.com*, accessed November 16, 2015. http://www.amazon.com/gp/product/B000WDY8U8/

16. "Charles Koch," *Wikipedia.com*, accessed November 11, 2015. https://en.wikipedia.org/wiki/Charles_Koch